Body Talk

Break It Down

THE DIGESTIVE SYSTEM

Steve Parker

www.raintreepublishers.co.uk

Visit our website to find out more information about **Raintree** books.

To order:
☎ Phone 44 (0) 1865 888113
🖹 Send a fax to 44 (0) 1865 314091
🖥 Visit the Raintree bookshop at **www.raintreepublishers.co.uk** to browse our catalogue and order online.

First published in Great Britain by Raintree, Halley Court, Jordan Hill, Oxford, OX2 8EJ, part of Harcourt Education.
Raintree is a registered trademark of Harcourt Education Ltd.

Produced for Raintree Publishers by
  Discovery Books Ltd
Editorial: Kathryn Walker, Melanie Waldron,
  Rosie Gordon, and Megan Cotugno
Design: Philippa Jenkins, Lucy Owen,
  John Walker, and Rob Norridge
Illustrations: Darren Linguard and Jeff Edwards
Picture Research: Mica Brancic and
  Ginny Stroud-Lewis
Production: Chloe Bloom
Originated by Modern Age Repro
Printed and bound in China by South China Printing Company

10-digit ISBN: 1 406 20414 5 (hardback)
13-digit ISBN: 978 1 406 20414 8 (hardback)
10 09 08 07

10-digit ISBN: 1 406 20421 8 (paperback)
13-digit ISBN: 978 1 406 20421 6 (paperback)
10 09 08 07

British Library Cataloguing in Publication Data
Parker, Steve
  Break it down! : the digestive system. - (Body talk)
  1.Digestion - Juvenile literature
  2.Digestive organs - Juvenile literature
  I.Title
  612.3
A full catalogue record for this book is available from the British Library.

This levelled text is a version of *Freestyle: Body Talk: Break It Down*

pp. 32-33 (Professors P. Motta & F. Carpino/ University "La Sapienza", Rome), pp. 28-29 (Sinclair Stammers), pp. 26-27, 36-37 (Steve Gschmeissner); Superstock pp. 4-5, 12; 14-15, (The Anthony Blake Photo Library/ Sam Stowell).

Cover photograph of man and apple reproduced with permission of Corbis/ LWA-Stephen Welstead.
The author and publisher would like to thank Ann Fullick for her assistance in the preparation of this book.

Every effort has been made to contact copyright holders of any material reproduced in this book. Any omissions will be rectified in subsequent printings if notice is given to the publishers.

The paper used to print this book comes from sustainable resources.

Disclaimer
All the Internet addresses (URLs) given in this book were valid at the time of going to press. However, due to the dynamic nature of the Internet, some addresses may have changed, or sites may have ceased to exist since publication. While the author and publishers regret any inconvenience this may cause readers, no responsibility for any such changes can be accepted by either the author or the publishers.

Dedicated to the memory of Lucy Owen

Contents

Mmm – yummy! .4

We're made of food 6

I'm hungry! .14

Stomach and guts 22

Want not? Waste it! 32

Total control 34

All under control 40

Find out more 44

Glossary 46

Index 48

Any words appearing in the text in bold, **like this**, are explained in the glossary. You can also look out for them in 'Body language' at the bottom of each page.

Mmm – yummy!

You enjoy a meal. You swallow your food and then forget about it. You may not think about food again until your next meal. But the food you eat will go on an amazing journey.

The incredible journey

Your food will travel through your body. This journey will take about 24 hours. During that time the food will be crushed. It will be attacked by acids. It will broken down into tiny parts. Your blood will carry these parts around your body.

Mealtimes are a chance to ➤ enjoy the flavours of our food. At the same time, we give the body the food it needs.

nutrients   useful substances in food that the body needs

What is food for?

We get **nutrients** from food. Nutrients are substances that the body needs. They give us **energy**. Energy is our ability to do or change things. Our lungs need energy to breathe. Our brains need it to think.

Food also gives us nutrients we need for growing. It gives us what we need to fight off illnesses. It also gives the body what it needs to mend itself.

Apart from this, we just love to eat!

Find out later ...

...how far you can run on an apple.

...what makes food "organic".

...how long it takes for food to pass through you.

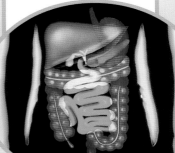

energy ability to do work or make things happen

We're made of food

Food supplies us with **nutrients**. We need these substances to stay alive and healthy. There are different groups of nutrients. Our bodies need a mixture of all of them.

Building the body

Proteins are one group. They are "building foods". You need proteins to grow. Muscles and other body parts are made of proteins. But they wear out. Proteins from your food repair them.

Meat, fish, and eggs contain a lot of protein. So do cheese, milk, beans, and nuts.

How much energy?

Different foods give us different amounts of energy. Energy is the ability to do things. Here is a guide to how much energy some foods give. It shows how far you could run on them:

Apple	500 metres (1,640 feet)
Slice of bread	1,200 metres (3,940 feet)
Portion of chicken	1,500 metres (4,920 feet)
Bar of chocolate	3,500 metres (11,500 feet)
Packet of peanuts	4,300 metres (14,100 feet)

Body language   **proteins** substances from food. They are used by the body for growth and healing.

Energy for life

Your body uses **energy** even when you sit still. It uses energy to make your heart beat. It uses energy to keep warm. It uses more energy as you move about.

This energy comes from food. **Carbohydrates** are "energy foods". They are often sweet-tasting foods like bananas, chocolates, and sweets. Or they are starchy foods like potatoes, bread, and pasta. Grains such as wheat and rice have lots of carbohydrates.

▼ Supplying people with food is a huge business. Vast areas of land are used to grow crops, like this giant wheat field.

Younger, older

Children need plenty of protein foods. They need them for growing. They also need plenty of carbohydrate foods. These are for rushing about and playing. Older people need less of these food groups.

carbohydrates   starchy or sugary food substances that provide energy

The "F" foods

Fats and **fibre** are two more groups of food substances. Fats are another source of **energy**. Small amounts of fats are also needed to keep some body parts working well. You don't get energy from fibre. But it helps push food through the body.

Not too much

Red meats like beef and lamb have lots of fats. So do milk, butter, and eggs. Some plant foods also contain fats. These include olives and peanuts. But be careful! Eating lots of fatty or fried foods can be bad for you.

These foods all contain ➤ plenty of fibre. Fibre keeps your guts working well.

fats   food substances needed for energy. But large amounts of them can be bad for your health.

Just passing through

Your body doesn't break down fibre. But it helps keep the **guts** working well. Fibre passes through your body. It comes out the other end and goes down the toilet.

Wholegrain breads and breakfast cereals contain lots of fibre. So do beans and fresh fruits and vegetables.

FATTY FOODS ARE BAD FOODS!

A new report shows again the dangers of eating too many fatty foods. Scientists think that too much fat can cause disease. It can cause diseases of the heart. It can cause diseases of the **blood vessels** (tubes that carry blood). It can cause disease of other parts of the body, too.

Don't get stuck

Leftover food and other bits in the guts form **waste**. The body needs to get rid of waste. Plenty of fibre in food helps the waste pass out easily.

Otherwise waste may get stuck inside us. This is called **constipation**. It is very uncomfortable!

---

blood vessels   tubes that carry blood through the body

Food minerals

Minerals are another group of food substances. Your body needs small amounts of many different minerals.

Calcium is a mineral. We need it for strong bones and teeth. Iron is another mineral. It keeps our blood healthy. Magnesium is also a mineral. Magnesium is good for bones, muscles, and **nerves**.

Vitamins

As well as minerals, the body needs **vitamins** to stay healthy. Vitamins are known by letters like A and B. We need vitamin A for healthy eyes and skin. Fresh fruits and vegetables are rich in vitamin A. Fish and

A pill a day

Eating lots of different foods should give you all the **nutrients** you need. But some people like to take a vitamin or mineral pill. They want to make sure they are getting enough.

minerals substances, such as iron, that the body needs to stay healthy

eggs are also rich in vitamin A. Vitamin C helps us fight disease. Fruits like oranges and lemons have plenty of vitamin C. So do many green vegetables.

A simple answer

The body needs about 13 vitamins. It also needs more than 20 minerals. Eating lots of different foods should give you all you need. Be sure to eat fresh fruits and vegetables.

Five-a-day
You should try to eat five portions of fresh fruits or vegetables every day. Of course, more than five is even better!

◄ Green for GO! These foods are very healthy. They provide plenty of the minerals and vitamins we need.

vitamins   food substances that the body needs to stay healthy

Too much

Millions of people around the world eat too much. They eat more food than their bodies need. Their bodies store the extra food. They store it as body fat. Some people become overweight. This can cause many health problems.

Not enough

At the same time, millions of people don't have enough to eat. Their bodies don't get the **nutrients** they need. So some people starve to death while others are ill from overeating.

Some plants and animals are ➤ raised for food in a natural way. They are raised without the use of man-made chemicals. These foods are often labelled "organic".

Special diets

The variety of foods that a person eats is called their **diet**. Some people like most kinds of foods. We say they have a "wide" diet. Some people don't eat meat. This is called a vegetarian diet. Some eat less food because they want to lose weight. This is a reducing diet.

Special meals

Sometimes people come together for special meals. These may be to celebrate something. It might be a birth or a wedding. It might be a special holiday (as below). For example, when do many people eat turkey?

I'm hungry!

Your blood carries sugar around your body. This is called **blood glucose**. It comes from foods that your body breaks down. Your body gets most of its **energy** from blood glucose.

Hunger signs

After some time without food, your blood glucose levels start to fall. Also your stomach and **guts** start to feel empty. Your brain recognizes

Regular supplies

Our bodies work best if we eat every few hours. Missing meals puts the body under stress. Then we are more likely to get ill.

blood glucose sugar obtained when food is broken down. Blood glucose is the body's main source of energy.

these signs. It realizes that your energy supply is getting low. You begin to feel hungry.

Ready to eat

As soon as you smell and see food, your body gets ready to eat. You get more **saliva** in your mouth. Saliva is also known as spit. It makes you ready to chew food.

◄ The sights and smells of good food make us feel hungrier. We lick our lips. We look forward to our next meal!

DID YOU KNOW?
You eat more than 12 times your body weight in food each year.

guts parts inside the lower body, such as intestines

Tasty! Smelly too!

Sometimes we don't realize we are hungry until we sit down to eat. Then we look at the colours and shapes of the foods. We smell the foods and taste their fantastic flavours. Our **senses** of sight, smell, and taste help us enjoy our food.

Early warning

Yeuurrgh! Our senses also warn us about bad food. It may look mouldy. It might smell rotten or taste odd. This food may be bad for us. It could make us sick.

Busy tongue

Your tongue is not just for tasting. It has other uses too. It moistens your lips. This seals them together as you chew. Then bits don't fall out. Your tongue moves food around inside your mouth. This helps you chew food properly.

Tasty tips

Many scientists believe that different parts of your tongue taste different flavours. (see below).

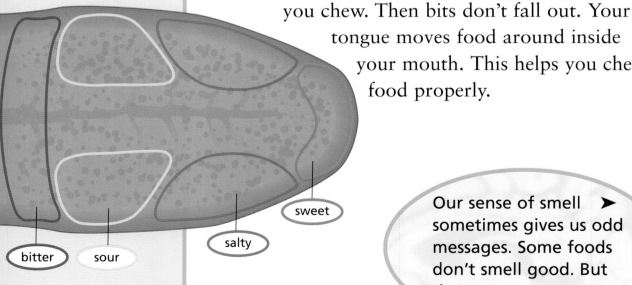

bitter

sour

salty

sweet

Our sense of smell ➤ sometimes gives us odd messages. Some foods don't smell good. But they taste great.

Body language   **senses**   the body's ways of detecting something such as taste, light, temperature, or sound

Spit, drool, dribble

Saliva is a watery substance. It helps make foods soft and moist as you chew. Saliva is made in six parts called **salivary glands**. These are inside your mouth.

salivary glands six small glands around the mouth which make saliva

Outside and inside

The outside of a tooth is very hard. It is made of a substance called **enamel**. Under this is **dentine**. Dentine protects your tooth like a cushion. The middle of the tooth is **pulp**. This is where you feel heat, cold, and the pain of toothache.

Terrific teeth

You probably bite and chew about 3,000 times a day. That's a lot of work for your teeth. But teeth are your body's toughest parts. They are about five times harder than bone.

A good start

The food you eat needs breaking down. It needs breaking down from big chunks to tiny parts. This process of breaking down is called **digestion**. Your teeth begin this process.

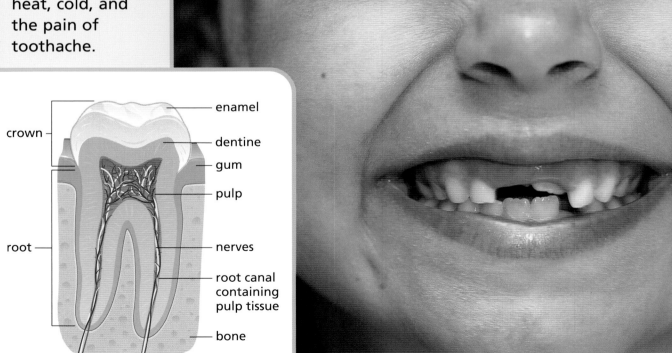

crown

root

enamel

dentine

gum

pulp

nerves

root canal containing pulp tissue

bone

    enamel   tough, whitish covering of the upper part of a tooth

Your teeth chop, squash, and mash your food. This makes the food easy to swallow. The more you chew, the better you **digest**. This means you get more **nutrients** from your food.

How many teeth?

By the age of about three, children have all their first teeth. There are 20 first teeth or "baby teeth". Then these teeth fall out naturally. Adult teeth grow over the next ten years. There are usually 32 of these.

◄ Once your adult teeth come through, you need to look after them well. The dentist will tell you how to keep this new set for life!

dentine   tough substance under tooth enamel

Swallowing

+ Your tongue pushes a lump of food into your throat.

+ The lump goes down. It goes past the top of your **windpipe**.

+ A flap closes over the top of the windpipe. This is called the **epiglottis**. It stops food going into the windpipe and choking you.

+ The lump goes into your food-pipe or **gullet**.

Down the hatch

You chew a mouthful of food. It turns into a mushy soup. This is the first part of **digestion**. But there is also another type of digestion. It is chemical digestion.

On the attack

Chemical digestion begins with the **saliva** or spit. Saliva contains a substance called **amylase**. As you chew, amylase breaks down food into smaller parts. It breaks down starchy parts like rice and bread.

Amylase is the first of many chemicals that attack your food. These chemicals are called **digestive enzymes**.

Soft and slippery

Chewing also makes food soft and slippery. Then it is easy to swallow. Try swallowing slowly. Put your hand on your neck. Can you feel the process shown in the diagrams below?

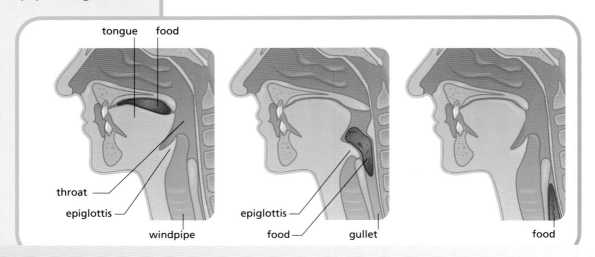

Body language   **digestion**   the process of breaking down food into tiny parts that your body can use

◄ Spaghetti goes into your mouth as long worm-like strings. But after chewing, it is mashed-up lumps.

gullet tube from the throat to the stomach

21

Stomach and guts

Self-defence

The stomach wall has thousands of tiny blobs (see below). These are called **glands**. They make gastric juice. They also make a thick slime. This is **mucus**. Mucus lines the stomach. It protects the stomach from gastric juices. Otherwise the stomach would digest itself!

The inside of your stomach makes a slimy, sticky substance. This is called **gastric juice**. Its job is to **digest** (break down) food.

Chemicals that kill

Acids are dangerous chemicals. They can burn skin. But there is a strong acid in your stomach. It is an important part of gastric juice.

Gastric juice also contains chemicals called **digestive enzymes**. These enzymes break down parts of food.

Acid and enzymes together are very powerful. They usually kill any germs that come in with your food.

Into a soup

Your stomach has strong muscles in its walls. They make your stomach squirm like a worm. This way the stomach squeezes and stirs the food. It turns food into a thick soup.

The stomach is not behind ➤ the bellybutton as many people think. It is higher and to one side. It is under the lower left ribs.

Body language   enzyme   substance that speeds up processes such as digestion

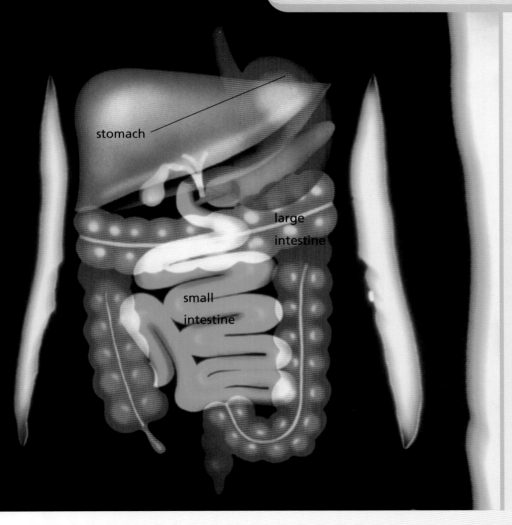

TIMELINE OF DIGESTION
This is how long a lump of food stays in each part:

Mouth	Up to 1 minute
Gullet	2-5 seconds
Stomach	2-5 hours
Small intestine	1-4 hours
Large intestine	10-18 hours

stomach

large
intestine

small
intestine

glands parts that make and release a substance such as acid,
   spit, or sweat

Next stage of the journey

Your stomach has turned your lovely meal into dark soup. This now heads for the **intestines**. These are long, tube-like parts. Food is broken down or **digested** in them. Intestines are in the lower body.

Smaller pieces

Your stomach squeezes food into your **small intestine**. Your small intestine is a little wider than your thumb. But it is very long. It is coiled up inside you.

Lots of chemicals go to work in the small intestine. They break food down into its smallest parts. These parts are called **molecules**. The molecules pass through the intestine wall. They move into your blood.

Pushing food

Muscles in the stomach and **gullet** push food along (see below).

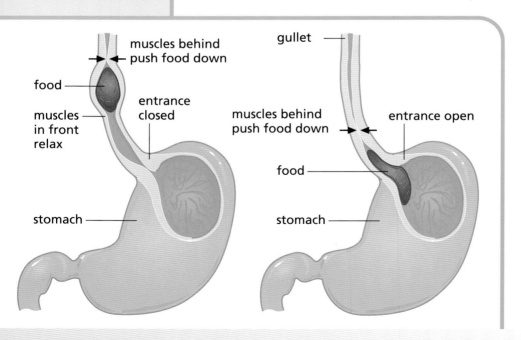

intestines   long digestive parts. They lead from the stomach.

Last length

Your small intestine leads into your **large intestine**. This is a shorter but wider length of tube. The large intestine soaks up water from the food. This leaves squishy, smelly brown lumps.

Straighten out

Your whole **digestive tract,** or passageway, is about nine metres (30 feet) long. The longest part is folded inside you. Imagine if your digestive parts were all straight (see below). You would need to be six times taller than you are now!

▲ The small intestine follows on from the stomach. This picture shows the inside of the small intestine.

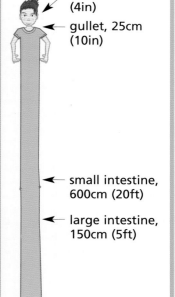

mouth, 10cm (4in)

gullet, 25cm (10in)

small intestine, 600cm (20ft)

large intestine, 150cm (5ft)

rectum 20cm (8in)

Powerful juices

Just behind your stomach is the **pancreas**. The pancreas is an **organ**. It makes powerful chemicals.

Juices from the pancreas flow into the **small intestine**. These juices contain more than 12 different chemicals. Their job is to break down different parts of food.

Soft and floppy

The pancreas (see below) is a floppy, wedge-shaped part. It is just behind your stomach. Pancreas juices pass along a short tube (pancreatic duct) to the small intestine.

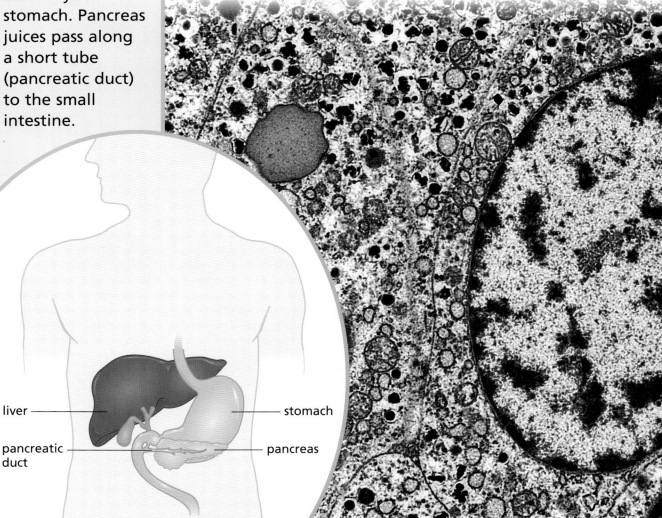

liver

pancreatic duct

stomach

pancreas

Body language   **organ**   main body part, like the brain, heart, liver, or intestine

Two tasks

The pancreas also has another job. It also produces **hormones**. Hormones are chemicals that control the way body parts work.

The pancreas makes two hormones. They control how much glucose sugar is in the blood. This sugar gives you energy.

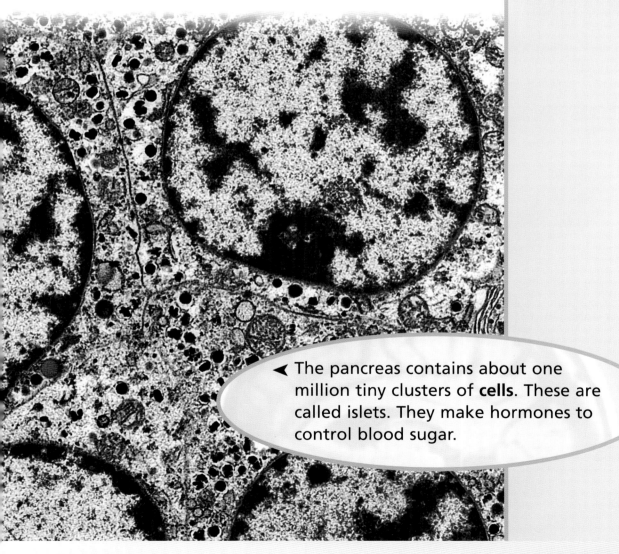

◄ The pancreas contains about one million tiny clusters of **cells**. These are called islets. They make hormones to control blood sugar.

small intestine   longest section of the digestive system. Most digestion takes place in the small intestine.

Inside at last

The **digestive tract** is like a long tube. Food stays in the tube until it has been broken down or **digested**. Then the food can pass through the walls of the tube. It moves out into the body.

This happens when the food is in the **small intestine**. This is the longest section of the tube.

Hairy guts

The small intestine is lined with about 500 million hair-like parts. These tiny parts are called **villi**. Blood flows through them.

Juices inside the small intestine break down food. They break down the useful parts of food (**nutrients**) into tiny parts. These tiny parts can then leave the small intestine.

The nutrients pass into the blood inside the villi. The blood then carries them away. It spreads the nutrients around the body.

More juices

The **liver** is just above the intestine. It makes a thick liquid called bile. **Bile** helps digest **fats** in your food.

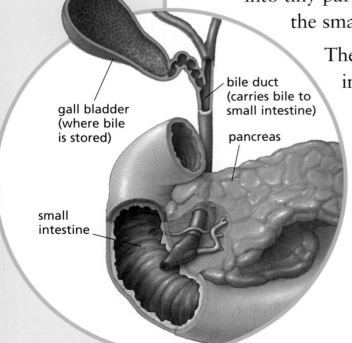

gall bladder (where bile is stored)

bile duct (carries bile to small intestine)

pancreas

small intestine

liver   large organ that adjusts levels of vitamins, minerals, and glucose in the blood. It also carries out many other tasks.

You can see food being➤ digested inside this jellyfish. If your body was see-through like this, you could watch your food turn into mush.

More and more
Tiny villi (below) line the small intestine. Each one is covered with around 5,000 even tinier "hairs".

villi tiny hair-like parts lining the small intestine, which absorb nutrients

Major multi-tasker

Can you do several things at once? Your **liver** certainly can. It has more than 500 tasks! After your skin, your liver is your second largest **organ**.

Changing, storing

Most of the liver's tasks are to do with **nutrients** from your food. Nutrients come straight to the liver. They come in the blood from the **small intestine**. The liver breaks down some nutrients into smaller pieces.

Blood red liver

Your liver is behind your lower right ribs. The liver is dark red. This is because it has so much blood in it.

liver

stomach

gall bladder

Body language   **organ**   main body part, like the brain, heart, liver, or intestine

These are easier for the body to use. The liver also stores some other nutrients. It stores them in case you don't get enough in your next meal.

Releasing

Sometimes there is lots of sugar in the blood. Then the liver stores some of it. Sometimes blood sugar runs low. Then the liver releases the stored sugar.

◄ A massive chemical factory produces dozens of substances. Your liver does far more. It also does it in a much smaller space.

small intestine   longest section of the digestive tract. Most digestion takes place here.

Want not? Waste it!

Your body needs to get rid of unused parts of food. It also needs to get rid of worn-out body bits. It gets rid of these things in two main forms:

• One form is solid **wastes**. These are also known as faeces. They are called plenty of other names too!

• The other form is liquid waste. This is called **urine**.

These two types of wastes are formed in very different ways. They are formed by different parts of the body.

Out at last

The **large intestine** makes solid wastes into soft brown lumps. Finally, the lumps are squeezed out through a ring of muscle. They end up down the toilet.

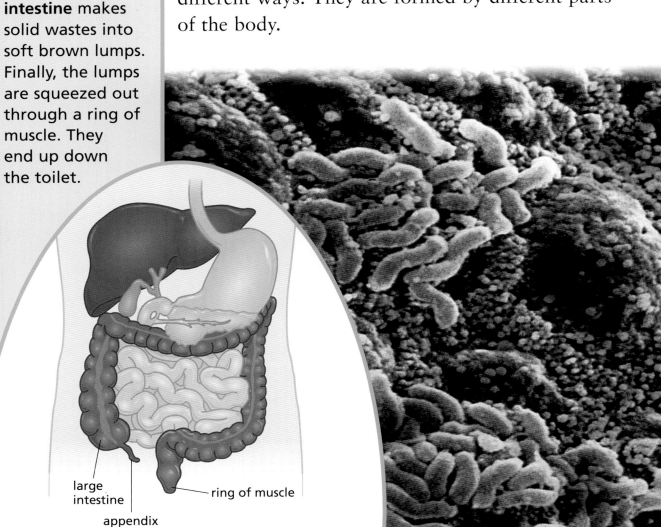

large intestine

appendix

ring of muscle

waste   material that the body does not need

Solids out

Solid wastes are made up of several things. They are made up of food that the body cannot break down. They contain lining from the stomach and **intestines**. This gets rubbed off as food passes through.

Another part of wastes is **bacteria**. Bacteria are tiny organisms. They help the body break down food. There is also water. Sometimes as much as half of the solid waste is water.

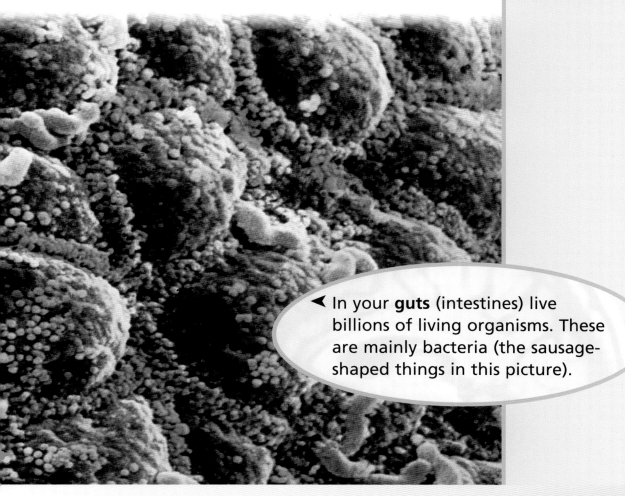

◄ In your **guts** (intestines) live billions of living organisms. These are mainly bacteria (the sausage-shaped things in this picture).

bacteria   tiny organisms. Some are helpful to the body, others can cause disease.

Total control

Urine is our body's liquid **waste**. It is very different from solid waste. It has little to do with **digestion**.

The liver has to do many tasks. Some cause the liver to produce a poisonous waste. This waste is called **urea**. Urea goes into your blood.

Making urine

The kidneys are behind your liver and stomach. Kidneys clean your blood. They also make liquid waste called urine. Urine travels from the kidneys into your **bladder**.

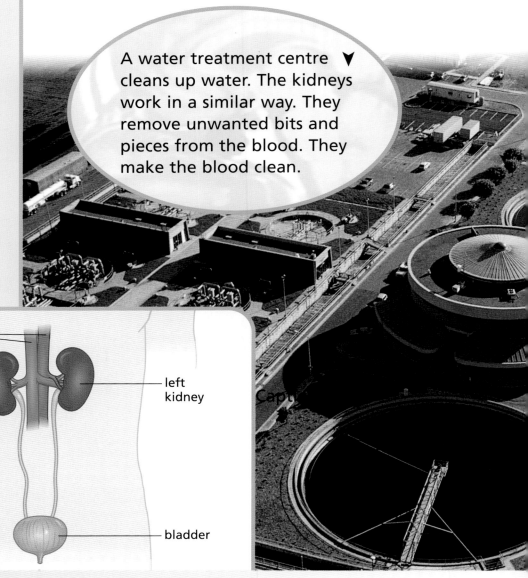

A water treatment centre ▼ cleans up water. The kidneys work in a similar way. They remove unwanted bits and pieces from the blood. They make the blood clean.

main blood vessels

right kidney

left kidney

bladder

bladder   stretchy bag that stores urine until it is a good time to get rid of it

Where wastes are removed

Blood travels around your body. It carries tiny **molecules** (bits) of food to your body **cells**. It also removes unwanted wastes.

On every journey around your body, blood flows through your two kidneys. The kidneys remove the urea (poisonous waste). They also make sure that you have the right amount of water in your blood.

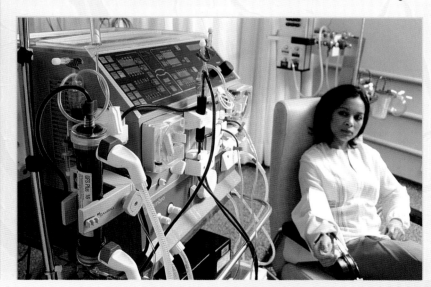

LIFE-SAVER

Some people's kidneys don't work properly. A dialysis machine can help. A tube takes their blood into this machine. The machine does the kidneys' job. It cleans the blood. Then cleaned blood flows back to the body.

molecule   smallest piece of a substance, such as a nutrient in food

Clean-up

Inside each kidney, blood passes through more than one million tiny parts. These are called **nephrons**.

Nephrons remove **wastes** from the blood. Nephrons also remove any water your body does not need.

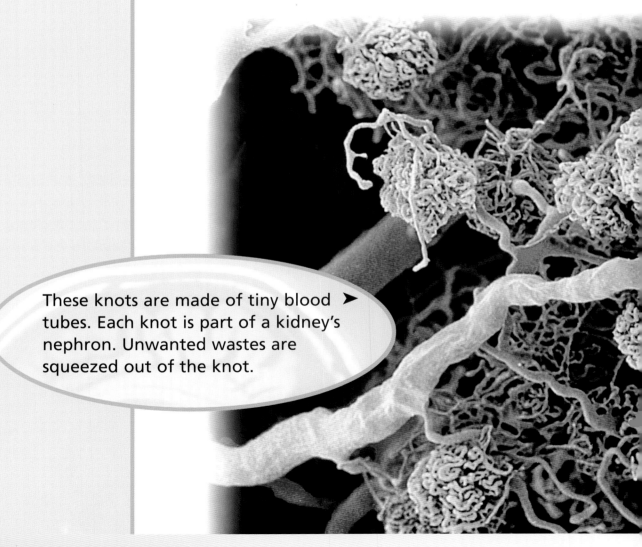

These knots are made of tiny blood ➤ tubes. Each knot is part of a kidney's nephron. Unwanted wastes are squeezed out of the knot.

nephron   tiny unit inside the kidney that filters, or cleans, blood

Watery waste

Water and wastes together form **urine**. Urine collects in a space at the centre of the kidney. From here it flows slowly down a tube. This tube takes the urine to a stretchy bag called the **bladder**. The bladder stores urine until you go to the toilet.

Night-time shutdown

The kidneys work fast all day. They work much slower when you sleep. Then they make less urine. This means you don't have to keep getting up through the night to use the toilet!

37

Holding it in

When the bladder holds about 250 millilitres (9 fluid ounces) of urine, most people feel a slight urge to urinate. By about 500 millilitres (18 fluid ounces) the need is desperate.

Weeeeeee!

Many people get rid of **urine** 10 or more times a day. This is called **urinating**. We also call it peeing or weeing. The **bladder** stores the urine. An empty bladder is about the size of your thumb. It changes as it fills with urine. It blows up like a balloon.

The need to go

There are tiny parts called **sensors** in the bladder wall. The sensors can feel how stretched the bladder is. The bladder fills up. The sensors pass this information to the brain. Then we feel the need to urinate.

sensor   part which detects something, such as sound, light, or a change in its surroundings. It then sends messages to the brain.

Letting it out

The **urethra** is the tube leading out of the bladder. You have a ring of muscles around the start of the urethra. These muscles relax when you go to the toilet. Muscles in the bladder wall tighten. This squeezes out the urine.

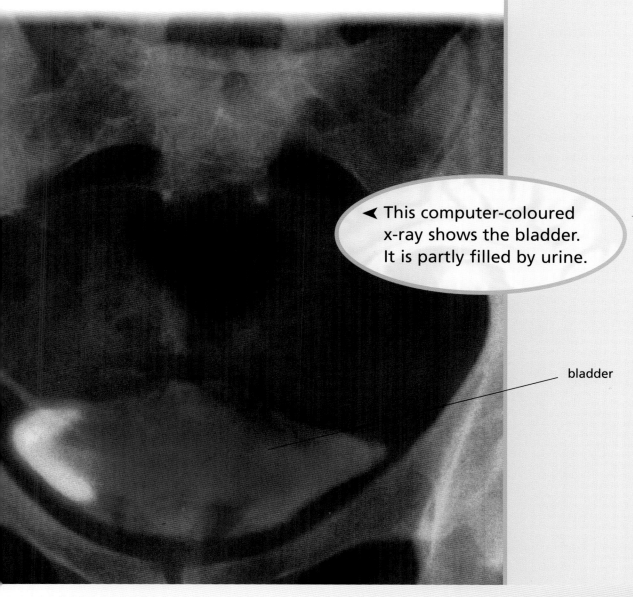

◄ This computer-coloured x-ray shows the bladder. It is partly filled by urine.

bladder

urethra tube that takes urine from the bladder to outside the body

All under control

Hungry, thirsty

When your blood sugar is too low, you feel hungry. When your body does not have enough water, you feel thirsty. These feelings happen in a tiny part of your brain. It is called the **hypothalamus** (see below).

Lots of different body parts work together to **digest** your food. Your brain controls all these processes automatically. This means you don't have to think about them.

Nerves and chemicals

Your body is controlled in two main ways. One is by messages from the brain. The brain sends messages along wire-like parts. They are called **nerves**. Nerves carry messages to different body parts.

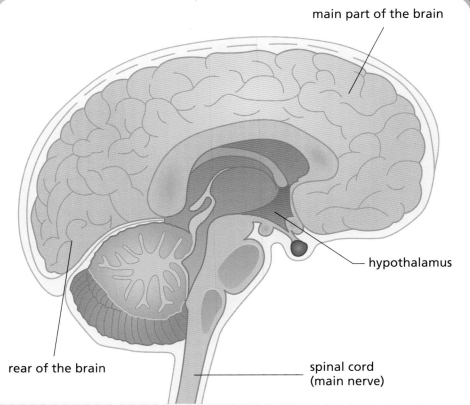

main part of the brain

hypothalamus

rear of the brain

spinal cord
(main nerve)

hypothalamus   small area at the front of the brain. It deals with emotions and automatic processes.

Your body is also controlled by **hormones**. These are chemicals made in the body. Hormones affect or control body parts.

Hormones and nerve messages make sure **digestion** happens properly. They also make sure that **wastes** are got rid of.

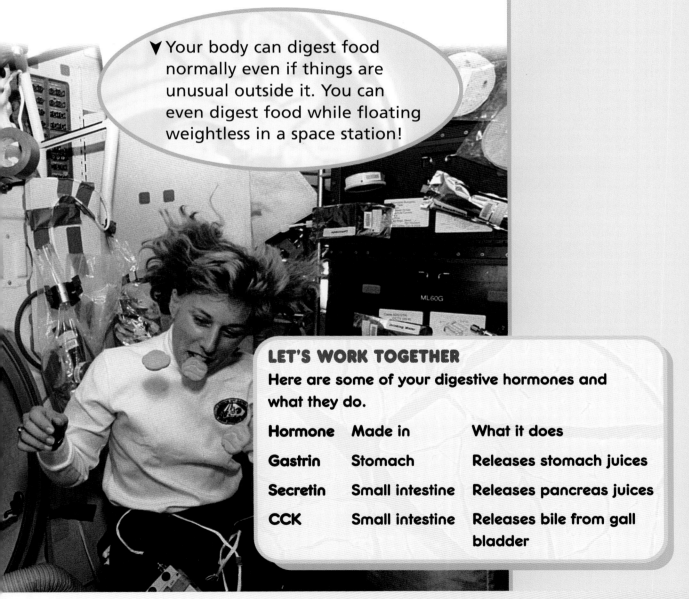

▼ Your body can digest food normally even if things are unusual outside it. You can even digest food while floating weightless in a space station!

LET'S WORK TOGETHER

Here are some of your digestive hormones and what they do.

Hormone	Made in	What it does
Gastrin	Stomach	Releases stomach juices
Secretin	Small intestine	Releases pancreas juices
CCK	Small intestine	Releases bile from gall bladder

I'm thirsty

About two-thirds of your body is water. Life cannot carry on without water. Every body part needs it.

More than four-fifths of your blood is water. Your brain is three-quarters water. Even your bones are one-fifth water.

Most people need more than two litres (3½ pints) of water a day to stay healthy.

Water in foods

Your food provides more than a quarter of the water you need. Some foods are more watery than others (see table below).

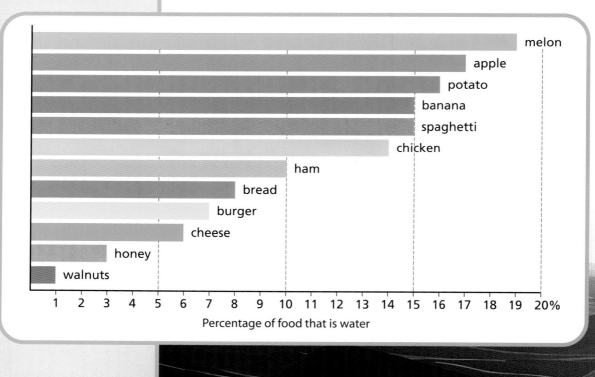

Percentage of food that is water

Where body water comes from

- Most people need about 1.5 litres (2½ pints) of water each day as drinks.

- About three-quarters of a litre (1¼ pints) of water is inside foods.

- The body makes its own water inside. Some body processes produce water. They produce a third of a litre (½ pint) every day.

Foods, drinks, and you

Drinking water helps you break down food. You can look after your body by sipping the right drinks and eating healthy foods. Food helps the body to grow and work. But first you must break it down!

◄ Don't ignore thirst! By the time you feel thirsty, your body already needs water. It works better if you drink small amounts often.

Find out more

Did you know?

Did you know?
The kidneys receive far more blood than any other body part, for their size. They weigh only 1/200th of the whole body. But they take almost one-fifth of all the blood pumped from the heart. This means your blood passes through your kidneys more than 300 times each day!

Books

The Digestive System, Carol Ballard (Heinemann Library, 2003)

Guts: Our Digestive System, Seymour Simon 2005 (Harper Collins, 2005)

Our Bodies: Digestion, Steve Parker (Hodder Wayland, 2005)

Body: An Amazing Tour of Human Anatomy, Robert Winston (Dorling Kindersley, 2005)

World Wide Web

The Internet can tell you more about the stomach and digestion. You can use a search engine or search directory.

Type in keywords such as:

- stomach
- nutrition
- saliva
- digestive system
- liver
- food

Search tips

There are billions of pages on the Internet. It can be difficult to find what you are looking for.

These search tips will help you find useful websites quickly:

- Know exactly what you want to find out about.
- Use two to six keywords in a search. Put the most important words first.
- Only use names of people, places, or things.

Where to search

Search engine

A search engine looks through millions of pages. It lists all the sites that match the words in the search box. You will find the best matches are at the top of the list, on the first page. Try **bbc.co.uk/search**

Search directory

A person instead of a computer has sorted a search directory. You can search by keyword or subject and browse through the different sites. It is like looking through books on a library shelf. Try **yahooligans.com**

Glossary

amylase substance in saliva that starts the breakdown of sugars and starches in food

bacteria tiny organisms. Some are helpful to the body, others can cause disease.

bile digestive juice made by the liver that flows to the small intestine

bladder stretchy bag that stores urine until it is a good time to get rid of it

blood glucose sugar obtained when food is broken down. Blood glucose is the body's main source of energy.

blood vessels tubes that carry blood through the body

carbohydrates starchy or sugary food substances that provide energy

cells microscopic "building blocks" which make up all body parts

constipation difficulty in getting rid of solid waste or bowel movements

dentine tough substance under tooth enamel

diet what a person eats regularly

digest break down food into smaller and smaller pieces

digestion the process of breaking down food into tiny parts that your body can use

digestive enzymes chemicals that break food down in digestion

digestive tract parts that food passes through, from the mouth to the end of the large intestine

enamel tough, whitish covering of the upper part of a tooth

energy ability to do work or make things happen

enzyme substance that speeds up processes such as digestion

epiglottis flap at the top of the windpipe

fats food substances needed for energy. But large amounts of them can be bad for your health.

fibre food substances that are not digested, but help the guts work well

gastric juice mixture of chemicals made by the stomach lining to digest food

glands parts that make and release a substance, such as acid, spit, or sweat

gullet tube from the throat to the stomach

guts parts inside the lower body, such as intestines

hormones substances made in glands and spread around the body in the blood. They affect or control body parts.

hypothalamus small area at the front of the brain. It deals with strong feelings, and automatic processes.

intestines long digestive parts. They lead from the stomach.

large intestine section of the digestive tract that follows the small intestine

liver large organ that adjusts levels of vitamins, minerals, and glucose in the blood. It also carries out many other tasks.

minerals substances, such as iron, that the body needs to stay healthy

molecule smallest piece of a substance, such as a nutrient in food

mucus sticky fluid in various body parts. It gathers bits of dust and germs. It also helps substances slip past easily.

nephron tiny unit inside the kidney that filters, or cleans, blood

nerves wire-like parts that carry messages around the body

nutrients useful substances in food that the body needs

organ main body part, like the brain, heart, liver, or intestine

pancreas part that makes juices for digestion, and hormones to control the level of blood glucose

proteins substances from food. They are used by the body for growth and healing.

pulp soft substance in the middle of a tooth, containing blood vessels and nerve endings

rectum end of the large intestine

saliva watery substance, also called spit. It makes food easier to swallow.

salivary glands six small glands around the mouth which make saliva

senses the body's ways of detecting something such as taste, light, temperature, or sound

sensor part which detects something, such as sound, light, or a change in its surroundings. It then sends messages to the brain.

small intestine longest section of the digestive system. Most digestion takes place in the small intestine.

urea waste produced by the liver

urethra tube that takes urine from the bladder to outside the body

urinating getting rid of urine from the bladder to outside the body

urine liquid waste produced in the kidneys

villi tiny hair-like parts lining the small intestine, which absorb nutrients

vitamins food substances the body needs to stay healthy

waste material that the body does not need

windpipe tube, also called the trachea, which carries air between the throat and lungs when breathing

Index

amylase 20

bacteria 33
bile 28, 41
bladder 34, 37, 38, 39
blood 14, 24, 27, 28, 30, 31, 34, 35, 36, 42
blood glucose 14, 27, 31, 40
bones 10, 42
brain 14, 15, 38, 40, 42

calcium 10
carbohydrates 7
CCK 41
cells 35
chemical digestion 20, 22, 24
chewing 15, 16, 17, 18, 19, 20, 21
constipation 9

dialysis machine 35
diet 13
digestion timeline 23
digestive juices 22, 26, 28
digestive tract 25, 28

energy 5, 6, 7, 8, 14, 15, 27
enzymes 20, 22
epiglottis 20

fats 8, 9, 28
fibre 8, 9

gall bladder 28, 30, 41
gastric juice 22
gastrin 41
germs 22
glands 22

gullet 20, 23, 24, 25
guts 9, 14, 33

hormones 27, 41
hunger 14–15, 16, 40
hypothalamus 40

intestines 23, 24–25, 27, 32, 33, 41
iron 10
islets 27

kidneys 34, 35, 36–37

large intestine 23, 25, 32
liver 26, 28, 30–31, 32, 34

magnesium 10
mealtimes 4, 13, 14
minerals 10, 11
molecules 22, 24, 32, 35
mucus 22
muscles 6, 10, 24, 39

nephrons 36–37
nerves 10, 18, 40, 41
nutrients 5, 6, 10, 19, 28, 30–31

obesity 12
organic food 12

pancreas 26–27, 28
pancreatic duct 26
proteins 6, 7

saliva 15, 17, 20
salivary glands 17
secretin 41
senses 16
sensors 38

small intestine 23, 24, 25, 26, 28, 29, 30, 41
smell 16
starvation 12
stomach 14, 22–23, 24, 26, 33, 41
stress 14
swallowing 20

taste 16
teeth 10, 18–19
  dentine 18
  enamel 18
  pulp 19
thirst 40, 43
throat 20
tongue 16, 20
toothache 18

urea 34, 35
urethra 39
urine, urination 32, 34, 37, 38–39

villi 28, 29
vitamins 10–11

wastes 9, 32–39, 41
  liquid wastes 32, 34–37
  solid wastes 32, 33
water 25, 35, 37, 42–43
watery foods 42
windpipe 20

Titles in the *Freestyle Express: Body Talk* series include:

Hardback   1-406-20414-5

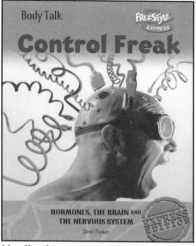

Hardback   1-406-20415-3

Hardback   1-406-20419-6

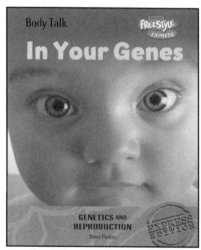

Hardback   1-406-20416-1

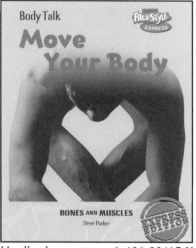

Hardback   1-406-20417-X

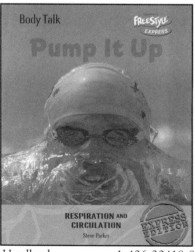

Hardback   1-406-20418-8

Find out about the other titles in this series on our website www.raintreepublishers.co.uk